ISBN-13:978-1503038264

ISBN-10:1503038262

Writing to Awaken

Tanka Prose
as Spiritual Self-Inquiry

Contents

Preface

This collection of tanka prose is a continuation of the work we started with Tanka Practice. Writing poetry is a practice for us, and tanka prose is a form that we have fallen in love with. Like the travel journals of Basho, prose allows us to describe the territory we have entered while the poem (tanka) hammers home perception with the crispness suitable to insight.

Our journey is a psychic one, and the territories that we encounter are the landscapes of our trials as human beings in this world. Unlike creatures, as humans we know our death is coming one day and we must face our terror. Poetry is the sword we wield, wrestling awareness from the morass of murky experience. As a group, we have chosen to work with words, and share our turning points with you.

For some time I have been working with creative writing practices designed to cultivate insight. While the purpose of creative writing workshops is to produce great, or at lest better writers, my workshops are designed to cultivate insight in the writer. Through the work of spiritual self-inquiry, my students (and myself) work to articulate our questions essentially and relay them in the most succinct and clear way possible. These writings retain the beauty of the individual writer as he or she undertakes the most spiritual of efforts-the effort of self-discovery.

Our goal is lofty and seemingly impossible. It is to awaken in this lifetime.

It is likely that the work of self-inquiry and clarity will produce better writers. Nevertheless, good writing, while the outcome of our efforts, is merely the byproduct of our purpose. We don't want to confuse the byproduct of our work for the goal itself. That our pieces are offered here is only as examples and to suggest the practice to others.

The forms of writing that I have used for this purpose have been tanka and tanka prose. Tanka is an ancient form of verse, predating haiku which it resembles. The tanka poem has five lines, loosely arranged as two haikus, one on top of the other with a shared middle line. In others words, in a good tanka poem, if you read the first three lines, you have a haiku. You will also have a haiku if you read the second three lines. While haiku doesn't include the "I" tanka does. Tanka has aspects of both the personal and the universal. This makes the form especially good for noticing the play between the personality and that which transcends the individual. Or, to put it another way, for those of us who wish to solve the mystery of how this one, the individual, is an appearing of the One as Self, it is the perfect form.

So in a way, I see tanka writing as a type of koan work. These koans are derived from personal experiences of suffering, joy, contradictory interests and so on. In Zen Buddhism, a koan is assigned to a student by the master. This koan cannot be solved by the intellect alone. Under the cultivation of the master and his or her own deep practice, the student may "solve" the koan and experience transformative insight. With the creative writing practice I am suggesting, the student discovers the koan that he or she is already struggling with as lived life. The writing practice helps the student clarify what are in effect personal koans.

It is a feature of my personality that my investigations are frequently stimulated by an observation of beauty. The observation is like a question for me which develops as I explore it. Here's an example. In Glacier National Park I notice a small pine tree growing on a cliff. Under the tree is a boulder with an uncertain future. It appears that a snow storm or wash of water in a heavy rain could loosen the boulder so that it could come crashing down the cliff. I take note of how the tree is reaching toward the sun and how it's twisted trunk reflects a long, slow craving for light. Already my words betray my projection. Am I the tree growing so precariously? How does the impermanence of the tree's situation speak to me?

I go on in my meditations. This particular small tree strikes me as particularly beautiful. Is that because it is alone? Is it because it is gorgeous even in the face of hardship? Or does the hardship itself shape the tree's beauty? Can they even be separated, the beauty and the hardship of the environment?

In tanka prose, the writer alternates prose with tanka. Often, the tanka seems to be of an entirely different theme than the prose and yet also seems to complete it. In our practice, we will use the tanka to bring the point home. The tanka and the prose go together, but seem to be slightly different voices. Sometimes I imagine that the tanka is like the Greek chorus of ancient theater. In our practice we shape this chorus so that it resonates as a question, or personal koan, or even the essence of an experience that the prose has already suggested.

By now, in our work, we have deviated some from traditional tanka and tanka prose writing. Since our search is a search for our true natures, we will be little bothered by that, but keep our eyes on the prize of self-inquiry. So we will bend the form this way and that, hoping that as we continue, an accidental artistry of our efforts will be born from the natural editor of truth and brevity.

angled against the wind
the tree and myself
cling to particles of soil
sun on our faces
this occasion of life

Leslie Ihde,
Upstate New York

What's New?

Nelima Gaokar

It is Tuesday afternoon. A temporary lull in the day's
activities has arrived. My co- worker walks in, sits
down, and says, "so what's fun, new, and exciting?"
My mind goes blank. I feel like he is asking about the
state of the universe, and I find it impossible to
answer. I have no entry point, no way to locate
myself in relation to the question. My cheeks flush.
As I feel sweat coming on, I wonder if I have any
deodorant stashed in my bag, certain that what I
smeared on this morning will not get me through
this conversation. There I am, limited being, trying

to find my way to the infinite in this casual talk. I
know full well that I am not likely to get there, but I
am stubborn. I want to say something real, not
something trivial. I want to use this opportunity to
connect on a higher plane...to speak at the level of
seeing, not unreflected being.

who is this one
with nothing to say?
my words truncated
by knowledge
of their inadequacy

No, it is not the words that are inadequate. It is I
who am inadequate.

I attempt to speak honestly, saying the question feels
too large. My co-worker looks baffled as to why I
would feel constraint with an open-ended question.
Finally he asks instead what I would do with a free
day. This I can answer. I would spend it working on
myself, making the effort to tend to my mind, my
body, my space. I would get outdoors and soak in
the bright skies and colors of autumn. I vaguely
reference yoga, meditation, and writing. He is not

satisfied with my answer. My careful speech and pauses suggest I am leaving something out. He is right. I did pause, wondering if I should discuss writing tanka. As I'm about to take the leap, he intervenes. The pause was too long.

my silence
an attempt to enter
the real
faced with a vacancy
the other closes the door

He asks about what he assumes I'm leaving out...my guilty pleasures. I follow his lead, and the conversation, though pleasant, shifts to a discussion of television dramas. I am mad at myself for letting another opportunity slip by...for not offering something more.

my silence misleading
I do not bother
to bridge the gap
mindful dialogue
still beyond my reach

Room for Beauty

Valerie Rosenfeld

My teacher talks me through my despair telling me
first this, then that, is not where I should rest my
head. I hear her voice calling through the fog and try
to walk, step after step to meet her, to meet myself.

After our talk she asks me to help her plant a tree.
Her kindness isn't lost on me and I say yes very
willingly. We plant the tree together. It is a Japanese
Stuartia, known in part for its mottled bark. I notice
the bark and the small green leaves on this young

tree and have a vague sense of its prettiness as I fill the hole with good soil. My teacher says the tree looks happy here. I look up and am struck by how true this seems. I have the sense the tree has found its true home and it knows it. A feeling of warmth rises in my body.

I don't understand it. But the tree all of a sudden seems indescribably beautiful. I feel its life and happiness in my own body. Can you love a tree? Yesterday I would have said no.

All the places I've rested my head, trying to get comfortable on a bed of nails. False solutions are discouraged and I stop. The world comes screeching to a halt. It is just me in my nothingness. In the nothing, first I feel dead, then just empty. Because of the emptiness I am available to be filled.

In the desert something shimmers on the horizon beckoning me forward when all is lost. Today I catch a glimpse of it. But it has always been there, promising.

mother's garden
little girl tugs her sleeve wanting
names of flowers
lifelessness
where dahlias are blooming

years later
in a different garden
not knowing
what I've been missing
~ room for beauty

My Marsh

Ellen Pratt

Every August, ducks appear in a small bog next to
the thruway. I see them on my commute back from
work. I enjoy looking at what they are doing, if a
great blue heron has joined them for the afternoon.
Often I will see a row of ducks on a dead tree
preening, while others gather sustenance from the
dark waters, their paths marked by the disturbance of
the algae. By October, they are gone and the marsh
seems so empty.

leaves blanket the ground
loons singing their departure
autumn is here
in all its glory to announce
winter is coming

In the marsh, a heron stands on a fallen branch. It's
cloaked in blue-gray feathers on spindly legs. The
heron rests, turned away and guarded in the shadows
of the trees. Nothing moving in the bog, everything
is still in the heat of the early summer day.

alone
I blame others for my
isolation
my teacher points out that I'm
self-isolating

I armor myself
so not to be penetrated
by the world
a chink ~ I turn towards you
and speak the truth clearly

I'm overjoyed to see the first duck of the season on the marsh. One day as I pass, I see it perched on a log; another day it's paddling through the algae exploring its home. Every day I pass, I look hopefully to see if other ducks have joined it. The duck preens and dabbles for food, seemingly unaware of being alone. I share with a birder my distress at this duck being alone; he explains to me that its mate is probably on a nest hidden in the grass.

I laugh
I'm my own victim
making up reality
instead of discovering
the truth

Rough Seas

Ellen Pratt

As I sit at Schoodic Point in Maine, I watch waves
crash on ancient rocks. I notice a tiny plover bathing
in a tidal pool. While I continue to watch, I see
there's a group of them feeding in and around the
pool, only being driven out when the waves have
enough power to reach them. But as quickly as the
disruption occurred, they are back again feeding
from the replenished pool.

I sulk again
others aren't aware of me
I retaliate
by refusing to see them
stopping - I return to my question

The energy of the sea can be felt in the air as the
waves break violently on the rocky coast. I watch a
pair of eider ducks float on the surface. I wonder
how it is they don't get thrown against the rocks by
the powerful ocean. Then I watch as they dive into
the depths of this chaos, coming up with a mussel
that they've plucked from the rocks below.

looking for myself
in unknown parts
I search my inner turmoil
for gems
and find peace

North Star

Valerie Rosenfeld

On September 11th, 2001 we were at our colleague's
house for a work retreat. I never liked work retreats,
where our therapy team would gather and discuss
the best treatment for our clients. I refused inwardly
to be a part of the team. I had always been like this--
afraid of succumbing to "group think" and wanting
to be able to think for myself-- and so I managed in
one way or another to separate myself, sometimes
with subtle hostility.

My boss understandably had a problem with me. I wonder if she would have been able to say so at the time but I think she knew deeply what I was doing and was angry at me for it. It was her team and she had poured her heart and soul and life into it for so long and here I was distancing myself from it and her with no small chip on my shoulder. She would speak to me angrily sometimes for no apparent reason. Unaware of myself and the effect I was having, I would tell her not to talk to me that way. But nothing ever was ever addressed directly.

hot and cold fronts
come from opposite directions
the storm in the offing
is preceded
by a strong wind

We had all gotten our bagels and coffee and were sitting down for the first discussion of the morning. Just after 9:00 my boss got a call from her husband saying that a plane had flown into one of the towers of the World Trade Center in Manhattan. As we thought about this strange and sad news, the day unfolded with a second plane crash and a third and then a fourth. And then the Towers fell, one after the other, before our unbelieving eyes. As the news got bigger and the ramifications grew clearer, we tried to understand what was happening.

For me the rest of the day was spent in a daze, unable to shake the images and the suffering, unable to see how I could continue to live in a world where people willfully, joyfully even, caused such harm on such a great scale right here in my back yard. How could I go on? I felt shattered inside.

I did not participate as much as others in cleaning up at the end of the day. My boss noticed this and said something to me. I said something about how upset I was and she said, "You know, it happened to all of us."

Before I left, her words were particularly curt and angry, again about something unrelated. I told her strongly not to talk to me that way. And then I left.

headlights
shining on the road
never shine
on the car
they come from

I don't know what made me then have a question.
Why Did she talk to me that way? Of course she was
right that "it happened to all of us." Why was I
acting like it happened more to me? Why was I
insisting on separating myself, elevating myself and
how could I not see how my self-importance was a
negation of her and the others?

Finally questioning my assumptions, I was able to
see the whole thing from her point of view and my
self-insistence fell away. Why was it so beautiful to
see as she did even though in doing so I discovered
my own egotism?

Overcome with guilt, I called her immediately. My
call went to her voice mail and I left a message
saying how terribly sorry I was to have disrespected
her and the others. When she called me five minutes

later, I thought it was in response to my message but she had not received my message nor even known I had called. The first words out of her mouth were "I am appalled at the way I spoke to you." I told her I understood why she did.

after the storm
clouds dissolve
back into the sky
without barriers
light pours in

Our separate insights, arrived at at the same time, seemed to still us. Why did this happen? Who was this person, who was I and how had we found each other? A sense of mystery and love remained where once two individuals stood. After that moment, I no longer separated myself and she was no longer angry. The love that arose in our moment of truth didn't fade and seemed present in our every meeting.

When my beautiful boss died recently, I was racked
with sorrow. But I felt my personal tears mingle with
those of countless others who lost her too. The void
she left happened to all of us.

night sky's Big Dipper
God's unwieldy ladle
doesn't deceive us
how else would we find
the North Star?

That Which Cannot be Contained

Esra Sarioglu

I was young, in my early twenties, when my peers began to talk behind my back. They said I was just a copycat, blindly imitating a girl I was close friends with. They were right. I talked, walked and even smiled just like my friend did. When she was not around, I took over her role completely, trying to be smart, original, and assertive. I didn't think that was a problem, until I had to face the mocking and gossip. Having shown the effort to be like my friend, I thought I could get what she got: attention and admiration. But instead I received diminishing looks and derisive comments. Trying to be someone other than myself was already shameful, but the fact that they did not recognize me the way I wanted them to be bothered me most.

capable
of incinerating it
burning flame
draws the moth
closer

A few weeks ago, I was at school to teach. Before my class starts, I went to the university restaurant to have a quick lunch. The room was almost full, but I managed to find an empty table. I sat alone at the small, square table set carefully with folded napkins, bread plate and silverware. Looking around, I saw a man sitting right across from me. He was around my age and like me, a part-time lecturer. We saw each other almost every week at the corridors of sociology department and said hi. I did not know his name, he did not know mine. I just knew that he was in the psychology department. He looked like a nice

person to me and I had a slight desire to be friends
with him.

He was eating casserole while peering at the screen
of his Ipad. During the lunch, we did not look at
each other, but sat very close. I lowered my gaze and
began to drink the lentil soup. As I moved up the
spoon to my mouth, the spoon suddenly felt heavier,
my grip became weak, and my hand began to
tremble. In an instant, I grew stiff. The next thing I
knew was that I was imitating the eating manners of
a friend of mine.

soft and vulnerable
things
like a naked heart
need to be contained
inside that curled wall of ribs

Then my grip relaxed, my movements began to flow
and I finished my soup. I was again at ease with
myself. I leaned back, feeling light, smiled at myself. I
was no longer angry at my twenty year old self, who

did not know how to be real in the world, in the presence of the gaze of others.

Sand Dollar

Leslie Ihde

We haven't seen him in a long time. He is middle aged now. His blue eyes are still soft but his words have changed. They are harder. He speaks about his sons. The older one, just ten, is not easy to get along with. I remember the nervous boy at five: thin and clingy. The younger one, four, is easier and more relaxed. This boy's eyes are soft brown like his mother's, but his temperament warm like Alonzo's once had been.

walking on the beach
our bodies float
horizon level
a flawless sand dollar
rests in my hand

He speaks about his marriage. Pretty bad. It would
be over if it weren't for the kids. She doesn't work,
and she's not much of a mom, but her parents are
rich. In his heart, Alonzo has turned his life away
from hers, so that the daily irritations barely matter.
There is the bankruptcy, too, although he is an
assistant professor. She spends, and her parents help,
but it has been a long, slow slide backwards.

I hand it to him
for his sons
and find another
smaller and perfect
so both boys will have one

I remember the man he was. Handsome-we thought
he could have any woman he wanted. He fell for this
one. "It takes two to tango," I think, but I never

liked her. Closed up like one in a dream. Her
reluctant smile the trap. Down cast eyes could have
been mistaken for shyness, but even then, I sensed
the door to her soul had closed. "Pity her, pity her,"
I chide myself in secret but I can't. I am angry for
Alonzo's lost life: lost in her pendulous breasts and
long, blond hair. Eve's apple in his pocket, just the
core now, he has fallen like every other.

he shows me
broken sand dollars
wrapped in a tourist's map
I think of giving him one more
but this time, I don't

In the Stillness

Allison Miller

In the group I attend, we try to discover who we
really are, to move beyond illusion. The teacher
points out to me, regularly, that I'm not clear when I
ask and answer questions about myself, and that my
lack of clarity keeps me in the
dark. Sometimes, her words are hard to hear. I want
to argue with her.

as a child
my skin was too sensitive
for the sun's light
as I've gotten older
I don't burn as easily

When I practice yoga, defensiveness falls away. I
notice the difference between a "well-articulated"
and a "foggy" pose — Awareness — and her words
begin to resonate. I notice what cultivates Awareness
— stillness, conscious breathing,
and questions. Are my arches collapsing? Are my
bandhas engaged? Am I lifting the side of my torso
while rooting my feet firmly into the earth? Have I
relaxed my shoulders, while engaging my legs? Is my
dristhi correct? What part of my body has not yet
been awakened by Awareness? What part of me?

listening
I discover questions
are vessels
defensive me dissolves
in the stillness of the pose

As practice continues, I notice another quality of the well-articulated pose — Alignment— alignment that feels almost effortless. There is a sense of ease in my spine, and integration from head to toe. I also notice that this alignment is not just physical, but that there's a deeper shift. The clarity that passes through the questions is now what I am. I become the clear space that questions and sees and at the same time I am the darkness being clarified.

her words come to life
on the yoga mat
the breath
finds its way
shaping and un-shaping me

Not One Shred

Valerie Rosenfeld

It is Sunday evening. I never see clients on Sunday but I can't say no to him when this is the only time he can meet. I want to help him if I can. He recently had surgery but was unable to take time off to heal. He works 12 hour days doing heavy lifting, all of it in pain from the swelling in his leg. His wound is constantly irritated and there is no time for elevation or ice or healing. His whole life has been like this. I notice as I talk with him how lost he seems, how sad his life is.

In general I keep some kind of distance with clients.
This distance is called "professional" in colloquial
speak but my distance is quite personal. I fear getting

lost in who they are. But I can't find my distance
tonight. Instead I feel acutely not how we are
different but how we are similar. He is in the dark
struggling to find light and also is also the one who
is in the way of the light. I feel in this moment so
terribly ordinary.

the emperor
not one shred of clothing
but he is warmed
by his belief in his
beautiful clothes

I can't imagine how I can help him. My distance
gives me the illusion of being a separate knower and
in this mindset I imagine (perhaps wrongly) I can say
helpful things. But tonight I am an un-separate un-
knower. We are in the same boat. What can I do?
But there he is closing his eyes, listening so carefully
to what I am saying.

blind men crossing
the bridge to the other shore
they can't see—
what will catch them
if they fall?

I have no idea if I help him. But he thanks me
sincerely as if I have. I look out the window and
watch him get on his motorcycle and ride away. I
lock the office door and step into the night. Though
we may think of it in different terms, I wonder if we
each leave with the same question. In all this
repetition of ourselves, do we have a chance to
break free?

full moon
ball of golden honey
on a close horizon
caught off guard
by its immensity

Red Book

Esra Sarioglu

I am holding a book in my hand. It is a red,
hardcover book called The Psychology Book. It
covers the history of psychology, beginning from the
Ancient Greek notion of humors to the
contemporary debates on emotions. I am hooked
instantly. I walk up to the checkout counter and pay
for it. The cashier gives my change and says, "Have a
nice flight," with a Greek accent.

Four of us are sitting by the gate, waiting for our
flight back to Istanbul. I am flipping through the
pages of the book, as if I am gobbling down a piece

of chocolate cake. I stop when my eyes catch "the four non-productive personality types" on the glossy page. Apparently, Erich Fromm developed this notion. Having read the four types quickly, I say, "Hey listen. Which one do you think you fit into? Are you receptive, exploitative, hoarding or marketing type? I read each type out loud. Both Irmak and her husband Jeff say that they might fit into the receptive type, a person who has no choice but to accept her role, and never fights for change or betterment.

I read the types again to see where I fit into. I glance at the exploitative type, an aggressive, self-centered person who typically engages in acts of coercion and plagiarism. It makes me turn my eyes away, as if it is something that I shouldn't see. My partner says, "Sometimes you might have exploitative tendencies." There is a note of nonchalance in his voice to make sure that I should not be worried or alarmed. I go quiet and my body stiffens. I look at Jeff and Irmak with anxious eyes to see what they have to say. They are kind enough to pretend that they did not to hear the conversation between me and my partner.

Back home, I am alone in the living room, sitting at the couch, reading the same page again. My partner is unpacking and putting some of our laundry in the washing machine. I fix my eyes on the page, thinking whether I am an exploitative type. My body stiffens again and I feel the rush of heat in my face. Then I take a long breath and say to myself, "After all, I exploit myself from time to time to meet some standards that I somehow set for myself. Why wouldn't I exploit others?"

I am surprised that my fences are down. Is it because I come to accept it gradually? Or is it because my consciousness opens up when the gaze of the other people disappears?

the evening sun lowers
over the Istanbul city skyline
its light softening
even the sharp edges
of the buildings

Breadcrumbs

Valerie Rosenfeld

I suffer in my life because I think I'm not real. I told my teacher this years ago. She assured me that she had heard of this sort of thing before and that human beings are trying to be real because they know on some level that they are not. I am not alone.

I suffer in my life because I think I am real. I go around asserting this. I'm real, you're not real. I'm real, why don't you recognize me? I'm real, listen to me dragging my feet through the leaves. Can't you see that I exist, that I am real?

If you treat me as real, I will dismiss you as being foolish for not seeing my unreality, my

incompleteness, my egotism. If you treat me as
unreal I will be angry at you for not seeing my
realness, my wholeness, my goodness. I will be
indescribably hurt.

at the kitchen store
I buy a red slotted spoon
perfect for keeping
what I want and letting the rest
fall back into the pot

Today my teacher questioned me. It was a day where
I was asserting I was real. She said *no, not as this one.*
How could she think that I wondered. *Can't she see how*
real I am? It takes me the full day to realize I've
projected one side. It takes me half the night to sit
and remember my inner contradiction.

I built the fire
in the morning
but there were no matches-
not til nightfall was I able
to light the flame

In meditation, first I have the fight with my teacher
in my head, then I return to my inner fight. I'm real,
I'm not real, I'm real, I'm not real.

if the apple
has a worm in it
it is rotten
eating around the worm
is not satisfying

I find myself praying for one word that isn't part of
the swirl. *Ok,* I say. *I give up. I Give Up. I'm not real.* I
say it without malice or self-hatred. Without sadness.
Just an admission. *I'm not real.* Silence and peace
follow. Claustrophobia gives way to space. If I'm not
real, what is this?

lost in the mountains
and the valleys
nonbeing
like breadcrumbs
leading the way home

Revealing this one

Nelima Gaokar

These days, I am rarely hopeful about a shopping expedition. The chances of finding something "right" seem slim. But I try to take advantage of the opportunity at hand while I'm in a place I've never been. After all, come Monday morning, I will have to put together another outfit in order to go out into the world. To not even bother looking seems wrong, as though I am turning away from something before becoming aware of what it is that I am turning away from. I browse through racks, trying to distinguish between my true rejection of an item and my reluctance to enter the question of what seems right and fitting for my purposes.

which shape, which color
reveal this one?
I am reluctant to find out
better to obscure the finite
than discover it

no, no...I am wrong
in articulating my philosophy
I have disproven it
my words necessary
to catch sight of my mistake

The Perfect Office

Monika Furch

For 8 years I have worked in an office with a vast view and great light, but a complete lack of privacy. The cacophony of many simultaneous conversations, phone calls and the constant coming and going, have made focusing on work difficult and quiet contemplation all but impossible.

Now, at long last, after having been promised a private office for years, one has become available. The office is immediately adjacent to my current workspace; same great views, but with a door for privacy. I am elated!

As the moving date approaches, a more senior co-worker decides to move into "my office" which leaves me with his darker, view-less space. I am appalled. I can't believe, that after having waited so patiently, with the perfect office within my grasp, it should be snatched away from me. In an attempt to change has mind and salvage my good fortune, I provide his choice of bribe; cookies, a different flavor each day.

Faced with the absurdity to which I have gone to preserve the "perfect office" for myself, I realize that this is about something more than just view and light.

Although I longed to work in a more quiet space for years, and either office will provide this, when faced with having a quiet space only, I come to see, that I have been attached to being in the center of activity and don't want to let go of it.

at long last
the large bird is given
a chance to fly
only by letting go of his perch
can he escape the cage

Curious Clarity

Allison Miller

I am on a writing retreat in Vermont, with a group
of lovely, perceptive, kind women. In the farm-
house kitchen we are getting ready for a trip to town,
where, as our retreat leader says, we will be like
Basho finding poetry as we journey through the
world. I am moving fluidly, until I am stopped by a
question.

packing food
for the day's journeys
for myself alone
or my fellow
traveller's too?

This is a familiar theme. In the past I have anguished at this apparent choice-point. This morning, a voice within offers guidance, instead of deadlocks. First, the voice asks, what is the actual difference between bringing just enough, or a little extra? Both monetarily and in carrying weight, it is not significant. The voice also reminds me that if someone is hungry, I will want to share, regardless of how much I have packed, so why not pack a little extra?

I notice that curious clarity guides me to an answer that works for this context; that starting from this awareness instead of attitudes that posit contradictions and seek timeless answers in the finite, inspires creativity.

the oil painting
of the large tree
at twilight
soft, muted edges
convey peace

Anchored

Allison Miller

We drive to the marketplace, from our quiet country
retreat house in southern Vermont. I have no desire
to leave, or buy anything, but when I see the fine
stores, and the people selling *homemade Vermont Pies,* I
become excited.

I don't even like eating sugar and gluten. But I am
fortunate, I know I am excited by the *idea* of a
homemade Vermont Pie, by what it means to me,
much more than the reality of eating one. This
knowledge saves me from having to eat it, and then
feeling tired and foggy — the opposite of the clear
energy I feel now.

victory
wielding the sword
of self-knowledge
illusory temptations
slain by seeing what they are

It's so nice to be here with my friends. We are poets, on a writing retreat, and have come to town "looking for poetry," not clothes, though I joke that a good sale is poetry! The night before we talk about the power of mindfulness. How being mindful gives our lives — our moments — the depth, richness, and even sweetness that we so often complain is missing. We wonder aloud — is it easier to be mindful in the country or the city? Some think it is easier in the country. That the city's distractions and temptations dissipate our intent. The question hangs in the air, is it true?

As I step into the marketplace, I remember this conversation. I remind myself that what I truly want is not in these stores. I do so in response to the "wanting excitement" that has arisen within me as I see them. The word equanimity forms silently on my lips, encouraging me to be so. This reminder helps me reject anything that is not in accordance with this intent, but also, to relax and enjoy it all. Throughout the day, I don't fall into any indecisiveness about what I want and don't want to buy. I notice this is the best time to go shopping. When I am not looking for answers in the wrong places, but rather seeking poetry. When what I'm buying is a condiment to the nourishment already found within. Anchored by my deepest desire as I try on the finely made warm, comfortable robe, and beautifully fitting winter coat, it is not hard to forgo buying them.

Relinquishing Ideas

Allison Miller

I see the eggplant colored fingerless gloves, and immediately try them on. I love the color. I know I need new gloves, and these are beautifully woven, made in Nepal, and seem to be of good quality. They fit well. I will buy them.

I happen to walk past a mirror as I'm browsing through the rest of the store on my way to the cashier to pay. They look ridiculous. The color is too bright. It is entirely clear black would be much better.

relinquishing ideas

when they are not in accord

with what is

graceful is the one who is

not attached to personality

Tipping Point
Ellen Pratt

Prior to showing a possible tenant the apartment on the second floor of my house, I do a walk through and become aware of all the flaws, such as the electrical work and painting that is needed. As I wait the list grows. Fifteen minutes go by and I notice the wall that needs shoring up and spackling. Then I see the window and door trim that is loose.

After a half an hour, I realize the young woman is not coming. At that instant, I feel the weight of my house and numerous things that should be done. The flaws have become me.

projecting myself
to avoid the unknown
I feign injury
facing the truth
the weight falls away

Invitation

Esra Sarioglu

I get off the ferry and see her standing by the port
in lavender jeans. Together, we walk away from the
sea towards the neighborhood hub. Today is the last
day of classes and I am glad to spend the night with
her outside, drinking and talking. I can not only talk
to but also listen to her, she takes living, writing, and
matters of inner world seriously.

It's Friday and we are lucky enough to get a table
outside. We order lots of things: fried calamari,
mashed broad beans, spinach roll, hummus, yoghurt,
beer, and Rakı. When talking about retreats and her
visit to Buddhist temples in Japan, the subject of
Trans Siberian trip comes up. We both want to take

that journey on Trans Siberian railway, the longest
one in the world, from Moscov to Mongolia, and to
China. We can make it; we can go to the center of
the old world. Both of us work part-time and she is
not a type of woman who directs all her efforts to
find a partner. Besides, I easily imagine myself with
her in a private train compartment, reading, writing,
and
watching the vast land and still lakes from the
window. The idea of being in her company does not
make me nervous. The only problem is money, a
problem which I tend to not to take very seriously
even though I am broke most of the time.

this soft spring night
crowds are pulsating
in the street
hidden
is the heart

After finishing her glass of Rakı, she tells me that
she stopped writing. "I don't even write in my
journal," she says. Once a successful engineer, she
quit her job last year to finish the manuscript of her

first novel, which the editor of a decent publishing house found promising. Tonight, she has a slight headache and looks a little bit tired.

I don't want to simply cheer her up, but give some hope. I mention my intention and effort to turn inwards. Upon noticing that she listens to me attentively, I decide to express how I sometimes feel about living. "This moment we are in seems to me a second-rate reality. The reason why I am doing what I am doing right now is because I can't go to that place, the heart of the matter. It is like a core, like a fireball and I feel its presence. But I don't know how to get there. So I keep doing what I have been doing." She looks at me, her facial expression is soft, but I don't know if she receptive to my concern.

at midnight
faint noises dissipating
in the silence I ask
what keeps me from this journey
beyond the ordinary?

The Longest Day of the Year

Esra Sarioglu

It is almost two pm and the sun is blazing hot. It
would be an arduous climb, so we decide to
hitchhike from the seaside up to the road in the
mountains where we parked the car. We are lucky, in
just a few minutes a blond woman with a slight tan
takes us into her car. Three of us happily fit
ourselves in the backseat. Our driver is Swede and
her car is rental. This is her sixth time in Lesvos. We
ask her if she has any suggestions on places to visit
on the island. She tells us to go to some beaches in
the north. "The sea is great, it is turquoise, but it's a
pebbly beach, she says. My friend asks me what
pebbly means in Turkish.

We don't have a Turkish word for either pebbly or pebble. There is a word "çakıl" but it refers to a kind of stone that has relatively sharp edges and its surface is a bit too coarse to be qualified as pebble. I explain my friend that pebbles are the small, round stones we see on the seashore. "Oh!" he says, nodding. The Swede woman looks at us through the rear view mirror and kindly repeats her last sentence. This time, she drops the word pebble. "You know it's a stony beach."

At the beach, I collect pebbles. My plan is to take them back home and put them in a ceramic pot on my writing desk. I hold them in my hand, looking at them in awe. Smooth and round, they are just beautiful. Waves gently break on the shore and as the water is pulled back, the hissing sound becomes more piercing. Pebbles continually rub against each other with the flow of the water. I know it takes a very long time for pebbles to take their shape. Waves incessantly move and stones stand still for thousands of years. Sometimes, beauty takes a lot of time.

I write, or to be more exact, I try to write. Words do not come easily. When they do, they feel neither round nor smooth. I wonder what my writing needs. More work? More time? I feel edgy. Compared to the lives of rocks and seas, my life is short. I worry that I might not have enough time to make my writing smooth and round.

With a few wet pebbles in my hand, I look at my friend. Under the summer sun, his face is relaxed; the quiet wind blows through his golden hair. Smiling, he asks, "Did you know that today is the longest day of the year?"

blue waters
a single wave crashing
onto the seashore
the longest day
refines the year

Dog Walk

Jennifer Werner

We walk Kiku together a few times a week, the dog
alternating between pulling to the front, the side, the
back. Sometimes she walks beside me, without
pulling at all, then I can be comfortable. She always
has a plan, a place to go, something to do. When she
walks beside me on the leash, I can move as I like
and so can she.

crossing paths
forced to stop, forced to go
being with others
side by side
aware or unaware?

Exercise for the dog is the reason for our walks. Tiring her out so she will be happy and well-behaved may be the goal, but talking about our future is the outcome. What shall we do about the girls' friendship losses? What's the benefit of this activity or that activity? What can we do to make their lives full and meaningful? What's the right thing to do, right now? Tugging a little, Kiku spots a dog in the distance and wants to make a friend. She brings us to the present. Our conversation can wait.

We go past the same houses and the same people as on other walks. I keep my eyes open for something new, maybe a different flower blooming, a home improvement project, a cat sitting in a window, and we continue our talk.

ideas and plans come
moving in just the right way
with action or without
we will arrive
at our future

Not surprisingly, we are again interrupted by empty
pleasantries with neighbors, brief encounters with
other dogs being walked, our own lamentations over
chemically-enhanced yards. We return to our
conversation as Kiku continues to meander,
switching between leading and being led. We pull
ourselves forward with no leash. I ask myself if we
need one, at the same time knowing how ridiculous
it would be to invite others or time to determine our
lives. Yet, I wonder about that leash. Would I
welcome one?

overwhelmed
by the possibilities
seeking internal direction
leading ourselves
looking for that one path

Primary Colors

Leslie Ihde

I always look for the primary colors that inform the
color of any thing. The cherry floor of my office is
red with tones of gold and soft brown. I review the
indigo, white, black and wine in my oriental rugs as
these colors dance tight arrangements of joy and
prayer. The multiplicity of the colors in the rugs
warm then shatter the room. In conversation, too, I
look for colors. The person speaking has a color.
Many, really. But I am looking for the hidden color,
the one the person himself doesn't know about.
Found under sadness, or anger, or circular
repetitions of thought, the person's hidden color is
teased from the blur of muddy experience. This

color pops like the red in my floor from grain lines
and brown. Familiar, like a friend, I see primary
colors revealed in their eyes; no, past their eyes, past
their talk.

a flicker of gold
on the side of the mountain~
brief reversal
dark sky, light earth
dancing spirit

Color is a yoga pose. Steady breath and gaze
centered by the command deep within. Deeper than
the person, deeper than the day, deeper than the life
that lives like a wave moving toward shore. The
crash is joyous and dreadful, the color of water
elusive. My eyes are steady. Perception draws the line
from ocean to shore.

movement
no movement
color no color
the ballet of water
slaps hard land

My uncle was the nice one. Favored by my grandmother for his sweetness, he lies in bed now, the final days of his life. I contemplate the gift that I could send him. Primary colors. The lucidity of spirit-blue, the flame of insight-saffron gold. Maybe he would want green life, turbulent and frightening, or the red heart of hunger. I will give him the color of water. Water when it is still and vast, love when it is depthless. Primary Emptiness. The peace that astonishes.

land on this shore
frightened one
I hold you
for minutes and years
in a flash of wonder

For more information on "writing to awaken" you are invited to contact Leslie at 607.754.1303 or

http://www.spiritualself-inquiry.com

http://innerartjournal.com

Made in the USA
Middletown, DE
24 December 2014